Rental Roadblocks:
Solving 12 Short-Term Vacation Rental Issues That Impact Your Bottom Line

AMANDA OTIS

OTIS
PUBLISHING

Contents

Introduction

The short-term vacation rental industry has seen tremendous growth over the past decade, with more property owners than ever before joining platforms like Airbnb, Vrbo, and Booking.com. The appeal is obvious: the potential for higher income, the flexibility of managing a rental on your own terms, and the opportunity to create unique guest experiences. However, as the industry has expanded, so have the challenges faced by short-term vacation rental owners. With increased competition and rising guest expectations, navigating the complexities of the business can be daunting.

In this book, Rental Roadblocks: Solving 12 Short-Term Vacation Rental Issues That Impact Your Bottom Line, we'll explore the top issues that can prevent your short-term vacation rental from reaching its full potential. These issues aren't just minor inconveniences—they can significantly impact your occupancy rates, guest satisfaction, and, ultimately, your profitability.

Each chapter of this book focuses on one of the 12 most common problems faced by short-term vacation rental owners, along with practical, actionable solutions to help you overcome them. Whether you're a seasoned property owner or new to the short- term vacation rental market, this book will give you the tools you need to stay ahead of the competition and ensure your property stands out.

We'll tackle issues such as low occupancy rates, market saturation, guest communication challenges, and property maintenance. You'll also learn how to handle negative reviews, address safety and accessibility concerns, and optimize your rental's performance by investing in luxury amenities and professional photos. In addition to these, we'll explore topics like legal compliance, damage and theft prevention, and effective time management.

As a short-term vacation rental owner (STVRO), your time, effort, and investment are valuable. Running a successful rental isn't just about listing your property online and waiting for bookings to roll in—it requires a thoughtful approach to management, marketing, and customer service. By identifying and addressing common roadblocks, you can increase your revenue, build stronger relationships with guests, and achieve long-term success in the rental business.

This book provides practical advice and expert insights to help you create a more efficient, profitable, and enjoyable rental experience. Let's dive into the 12 common roadblocks that may be holding you back and discover how to solve them in a way that positively impacts your bottom line.

Chapter 1 - STVRO Problem #1: Low Occupancy Rates in Short-Term Rentals

Low occupancy rates are a common challenge for short-term vacation rental owners (STVROs), impacting profitability and long-term success. However, there are proven strategies to attract more bookings and maintain a steady flow of guests year-round. By combining smart pricing, marketing, and guest engagement tactics, rental owners can maximize their property's potential.

Optimize Pricing with Dynamic Pricing Tools

Dynamic pricing tools like Beyond Pricing, Wheelhouse, or PriceLabs analyze market trends, local demand, and competition to adjust nightly rates in real-time. These tools ensure your property remains competitively priced, attracting bookings without undervaluing your rental. Proper pricing can significantly boost occupancy, especially during peak and off-peak seasons.

Invest in Targeted Digital Marketing Campaigns

Running digital marketing campaigns through platforms like Google Ads, Facebook, and Instagram can help you reach potential guests directly. Use high-quality visuals and compelling messaging to showcase your property's unique features. Targeting specific demographics, such as families or business travelers, can further increase visibility and bookings.

List on Multiple Booking Platforms

Relying on a single platform like Airbnb can limit your reach. Expand your audience by listing on multiple booking platforms like Vrbo and Booking.com and niche sites like Plum Guide or Kid & Coe. This increases the chances of your property being discovered by a wider range of travelers.

Improve Property Descriptions and Titles for SEO

A well-crafted property description optimized for search engines can significantly boost visibility. Use key words that travelers will likely search for, such as "beachfront villa with private pool" or "cozy cabin near hiking trails." Highlight amenities, nearby attractions, and unique features in a concise and engaging way to capture attention.

Offer Discounts for Long-Term Stays or Off-Season Bookings

Encouraging longer stays with discounted rates can fill gaps in your calendar and reduce turnover costs. Similarly, offering off-season promotions attracts budget-conscious travelers during slower periods. These strategies keep your property occupied while generating a steady income.

Utilize Local Partnerships for Referrals

Partnering with local businesses such as restaurants, tour operators, and event planners can create mutually beneficial referral systems. For example, offering discounts to guests referred by a nearby business can drive bookings while supporting the local community.

Host Unique Events or Experiences

Stand out from the competition by hosting on-site events or experiences, such as cooking classes, wine tastings, or yoga sessions. These offerings attract guests seeking more than just a place to stay and add value to their experience, boosting both occupancy and satisfaction.

Encourage Repeat Bookings with Loyalty Programs

Rewarding repeat guests with discounts, early check-ins, or exclusive perks can foster loyalty and increase direct bookings. A simple loyalty program incentivizes past guests to return and reduces reliance on booking platform commissions.

Analyze Competitors' Strategies and Adjust Offerings

Regularly reviewing competitors' pricing, amenities, and marketing strategies can help you stay competitive. If similar properties offer features like free parking or complimentary breakfast, consider adding those to your listing to remain competitive.

Highlight Unique Selling Points

Your property's unique features, such as its location, design, or unique amenities, should be prominently showcased in your listing. Whether it's a rooftop deck with stunning views or proximity to popular attractions, emphasizing what sets your property apart can draw more interest.

By implementing these solutions, short-term vacation rental owners can tackle low occupancy rates effectively, attract more guests, and increase revenue. The key is staying proactive, understanding market trends, and consistently enhancing the guest experience.

Chapter 2- STVRO Problem #2: Market Saturation in the Short-Term Rental Industry

Overcoming Market Saturation in the Short-Term Vacation Rental Industry

Market saturation is a growing challenge in the short-term vacation rental industry as the number of properties increases, making it harder for individual rentals to stand out. However, with a strategic approach, property owners can differentiate themselves, attract more bookings, and remain competitive.

Identify and Target Niche Markets

Focusing on niche markets can help your property stand out in a crowded marketplace. Cater to specific guest needs, such as pet-friendly accommodations, family-friendly amenities, or properties designed for remote workers. Tailoring your property to a particular audience creates a competitive edge and attracts loyal guests.

Emphasize Local and Cultural Experiences

Travelers often seek authentic experiences unique to the destination. Highlight opportunities for guests to explore local cultures, such as nearby festivals, artisanal markets, or regional cuisine. Providing guides, discounts, or partnerships with local businesses adds value to their stay and sets your property apart.

Offer Personalized Guest Services

Guests appreciate thoughtful, tailored touches. Offer personalized services like welcome baskets with local treats, customized itineraries, or pre-arrival grocery shopping. Such gestures create a memorable experience, encouraging positive reviews and repeat bookings.

Invest in Branding and Professional Property Presentation

A strong brand identity can make your property more recognizable and appealing. Invest in professional photography, a memorable logo, and consistent design across listings and marketing materials. A well-branded property conveys quality and professionalism, helping it stand out in a saturated market.

Highlight Eco-Friendly or Sustainable Practices

As more travelers prioritize sustainability, showcasing your eco-friendly efforts can attract environmentally conscious guests. Features like energy-efficient appliances, recycling options, and sustainable toiletries make your property more appealing while demonstrating your commitment to the planet.

Use Customer Testimonials to Stand Out

Guest reviews and testimonials are powerful tools for building trust and credibility. Highlight glowing feedback about your property's cleanliness, amenities, or unique features in your listing and marketing materials. Social proof can set you apart from competitors with similar offerings.

Build Relationships with Travel Bloggers and Influencers

Collaborating with influencers or travel bloggers can significantly boost your rental property's visibility. Host them for a stay in exchange for promotional content, such as blog posts, Instagram features, or YouTube videos. Their endorsement introduces your property to a broader audience.

Enhance Guest Retention Strategies

Encouraging repeat bookings is an effective way to reduce dependency on new guests. Offer returning guests discounts loyalty rewards, or special perks to secure continued business. Repeat guests not only fill your calendar but also provide referrals and positive reviews.

Rebrand with Unique Property Themes or Décor

A themed property can transform a standard listing into a must-visit destination. Consider creating a cozy cabin retreat, a vintage-inspired getaway, or a modern luxury escape. Unique décor and design make your property memorable and shareable on social media, increasing its appeal.

Create Value Bundles

Bundling extra perks like free parking, attraction tickets, or complimentary breakfast can differentiate your listing from others in the same price range. These value-added offerings give guests more for their money and create a sense of exclusivity.

Market saturation may seem daunting, but it also creates an opportunity to innovate and excel. Property owners can carve out a unique identity in the short-term vacation rental landscape by targeting niche markets, enhancing guest experiences, and investing in professional branding. These strategies help you stand out and build guest loyalty, ensuring long-term success.

Chapter 3- STVRO Problem #3: Guest Communication Issues

Addressing Guest Communication Issues in Short-Term Rentals

Guest communication is the backbone of a successful short-term vacation rental experience. Poor communication can lead to misunderstandings, negative reviews, and lost bookings, while effective communication fosters trust, ensures guest satisfaction, and encourages repeat stays.

Implement Automated Messaging for Booking Confirmations and Check-Ins

Automated messaging systems streamline communication by sending guests timely updates, such as booking confirmations, check-in instructions, and reminders. Tools like Hostfully and Guesty can automate these processes, ensuring guests receive the necessary information without delays.

Use Chatbots for Quick Responses

Chatbots are an excellent solution for handling common guest queries around the clock. By integrating chatbots into your website or booking platform, guests can get instant answers to frequently asked questions, such as check-in times, Wi-Fi passwords, or parking details.

Offer 24/7 Support with a Virtual Assistant or Call Service

Guests often have questions or issues outside of regular business hours. Providing 24/7 support through a virtual assistant or a dedicated call service ensures that someone is always available to address their needs promptly, enhancing the guest experience and building trust.

Provide a Detailed Guest Manual

A comprehensive guest manual is a valuable resource for your guests. It should include details about the property, check-in and check-out procedures, house rules, local attractions, emergency contacts, and appliance troubleshooting tips. A well-organized manual reduces the need for repetitive inquiries.

Ensure Clear Communication of House Rules

Clearly stating house rules before guests arrive prevents misunderstandings. Include these in your booking confirmation emails, the guest manual, and your property listing. Clearly communicated rules help set expectations and maintain harmony during their stay.

Train Staff for Effective Customer Service

If you have staff managing guest interactions, invest in customer service training to ensure they communicate clearly, professionally, and empathetically. Staff members who can handle guest concerns courteously and efficiently enhance the overall experience and protect your property's reputation.

Use Pre-Stay Surveys to Anticipate Needs

Sending a pre-stay survey allows you to gather information about guests' preferences and requirements. Whether they need a crib, dietary recommendations, or extra towels, anticipating their needs demonstrates care and can result in glowing reviews.

Include FAQs on Your Booking Site

An FAQ section on your short-term vacation rental booking platform or website addresses common concerns like refund policies, pet policies, and parking availability. This not only saves time for guests but also reduces the volume of repetitive inquiries.

Offer Multilingual Support if Targeting International Guests

If you attract international travelers, consider offering multilingual support. Automated translation tools, multilingual staff, or professionally translated materials can bridge language barriers and make your property more accessible to a global audience.

Respond Promptly and Politely to Guest Inquiries

Timely and polite responses to guest questions or concerns show professionalism and respect. Aim to respond within a few hours, if not immediately. Even when facing challenges, maintaining a polite and solution-focused tone ensures guests feel valued.

Effective communication is essential for providing a seamless and enjoyable short-term rental experience. By implementing these solutions, rental owners can address common communication issues, build stronger relationships with guests, and ultimately increase bookings and positive reviews. Clear, timely, thoughtful communication improves guest satisfaction and strengthens your property's reputation in a competitive market.

Chapter 4- STVRO Problem #4: Property Maintenance and Cleanliness

The Importance of Property Maintenance and Cleanliness in Short-Term Rentals

Property maintenance and cleanliness are critical factors in the success of any short-term rental business. A well-maintained and impeccably clean property enhances guest satisfaction, earns positive reviews, and ensures repeat bookings. Neglecting these aspects, however, can lead to dissatisfied guests, negative feedback, and potential loss of revenue.

Schedule Regular Deep Cleaning

Deep cleaning ensures your property remains spotless and inviting, going beyond surface-level tidying. Schedule thorough cleanings at least once a month to address areas that standard cleanings may overlook, such as carpets, upholstery, and air vents. Guests will appreciate the fresh, well-kept environment.

Create a Maintenance Checklist

A detailed maintenance checklist helps you stay organized and proactive. Include tasks like testing smoke detectors, checking HVAC systems, inspecting plumbing for leaks, and monitoring appliance performance. Regularly updating this list ensures no detail is overlooked.

Hire Reliable Cleaning and Maintenance Staff

Reliable and skilled staff are essential for keeping your property in top condition. Partner with professional cleaning services and maintenance teams who understand the specific needs of short-term rentals and can provide consistent, high-quality work.

Conduct Frequent Inspections

Frequent property inspections allow you to catch potential issues before they escalate. Walk through the property regularly to check for wear and tear, cleanliness, and any safety hazards. Inspections ensure your property is always guest-ready.

Use Professional Pest Control Services

Pests can quickly tarnish your rental's reputation. Schedule regular pest control services to prevent infestations and reassure guests of a clean and safe environment. Professional services also address potential problems that DIY solutions might miss.

Replace Worn-Out Items Promptly

Worn-out furniture, bedding, or appliances detract from the guest experience. Replace these items as soon as they show signs of wear. Investing in quality replacements demonstrates your commitment to guest comfort and satisfaction.

Offer a Cleaning Service for Long-Term Guests

For extended stays, offer mid-stay cleaning services to ensure the property remains clean and inviting. Guests will appreciate the added convenience, and your property will stay in better condition throughout their stay.

Partner with Local Vendors for Repairs

Building relationships with local vendors ensures you have a reliable network for quick repairs. Whether it's plumbing, electrical work, or appliance servicing, having trusted professionals on call minimizes downtime and disruption for guests.

Invest in Durable, Easy-to-Clean Materials

Choose durable and low-maintenance materials, such as vinyl flooring, washable paint, and stain-resistant fabrics. These materials reduce cleaning time and maintenance costs while ensuring the property looks polished.

Use Technology to Track Maintenance Schedules

Leverage technology to streamline your maintenance efforts. Property management software and apps like Breezeway or Hostfully can help you track cleaning schedules, log inspections, and receive maintenance alerts, ensuring nothing is missed.

Maintaining a clean and well-cared-for property is vital to the success of your short-term rental. Implementing these strategies keeps your property in excellent condition and enhances guest satisfaction, leading to positive reviews and increased bookings. By prioritizing maintenance and cleanliness, you protect your investment, build your reputation, and secure long-term profitability in the competitive short-term rental market.

Chapter 5- STVRO Problem #5: 5. Comparable and Luxury Amenities

Enhancing Guest Experiences with Comparable and Luxury Amenities in Short-Term Rentals

In today's competitive short-term vacation rental market, offering exceptional amenities is essential to attracting guests, earning positive reviews, and securing repeat bookings. Comparable and luxury amenities can set your property apart, creating memorable stays that drive profitability. Guests increasingly expect rentals to offer the same conveniences and comforts as high-end hotels, and delivering on these expectations can significantly boost your rental's appeal.

Add High-Quality Bedding and Linens

Investing in premium bedding and linens instantly elevates the guest experience. Soft, high-thread-count sheets, plush pillows, and cozy comforters create a hotel-like atmosphere.

Clean, fresh-smelling linens add a touch of luxury that guests will appreciate.

Include Smart Home Features Like Keyless Entry

Smart home technology adds convenience and a modern touch to your rental. Keyless entry systems provide secure and hassle-free check-ins, while features like smart thermostats and voice-activated assistants enhance comfort and convenience.

Provide Streaming Services and High-Speed Wi-Fi

Guests expect seamless connectivity during their stay. Offering high-speed Wi-Fi and access to popular streaming services like Netflix, Hulu, or Disney+ ensures entertainment options for all guests, particularly families and remote workers.

Stock Kitchens with Modern Appliances

A well-equipped kitchen can be a major selling point. Include modern appliances like coffee makers, blenders, and toasters, along with quality cookware and utensils. Stocking the kitchen with essentials such as coffee pods and spices adds an extra layer of convenience.

Offer Complimentary Toiletries

Small touches like complimentary toiletries can leave a lasting impression. Provide high-quality shampoo, conditioner, body wash, and lotion. Eco-friendly, sustainably packaged products can appeal to environmentally conscious travelers.

Add Outdoor Amenities Like Fire Pits or BBQs

Outdoor spaces are a significant draw for guests. Install features like a fire pit, BBQ grill, or comfortable seating to create inviting areas for relaxation or socializing. These amenities are desirable for families or groups.

Install Energy-Efficient Lighting

Energy-efficient LED lighting reduces utility costs and enhances the ambiance of your property. Use warm, dimmable lights to create a cozy and inviting atmosphere for guests.

Include Extras Like Bikes or Beach Gear

Providing extras like bicycles, kayaks, or beach gear can differentiate your property and attract niche markets, such as outdoor enthusiasts or beachgoers. These amenities also encourage guests to explore and enjoy the local area.

Provide Luxury Touches Like a Welcome Gift or Snack Basket

A thoughtful welcome gift, such as a snack basket or bottle of wine, sets a positive tone for the stay. Personalized notes or locally sourced treats can make guests feel valued and create memorable experiences.

Survey Guests to Understand Desired Amenities

Guest feedback is invaluable for identifying desired amenities. Use surveys to understand what your target audience values most, allowing you to make informed decisions about upgrades and investments.

Adding comparable and luxury amenities to your short-term rental enhances guest satisfaction and increases your property's perceived value. By incorporating thoughtful touches and modern conveniences, you can attract more bookings, stand out in a competitive market, and maximize your revenue. Whether through high-quality bedding, smart technology, or unique outdoor features, investing in exceptional amenities pays off in the form of happier guests and long-term profitability.

Chapter 6- STVRO Problem #6: Dark, Old, or Inaccurate Photographs

The Importance of High-Quality Photography for Short-Term Vacation Rentals

The saying "a picture is worth a thousand words" holds especially true in short-term rentals. Dark, outdated, or inaccurate photographs can deter potential guests, lower booking rates, and impact revenue. With most travelers relying on online listings to choose accommodations, high-quality, appealing photos are critical in standing out.

Hire a Professional Short-Term Rental Photographer

Investing in a professional photographer specializing in real estate or vacation rentals is one of the best ways to showcase your property. Professionals understand how to capture the best angles, lighting, and composition, ensuring your property looks inviting and spacious.

Use Bright, Natural Lighting for Photos

Bright and well-lit images create a welcoming atmosphere. Schedule your photoshoot during daylight, preferably when the property receives ample natural light. Avoid harsh shadows or overly bright reflections by diffusing sunlight with sheer curtains.

Stage the Property with Appealing Décor

Staging your property with tasteful and appealing décor can elevate its visual appeal. Arrange furniture to optimize space, add pops of color with cushions or flowers, and create a cohesive style that resonates with your target audience. Use props or people to create scenes portraying what guests will experience during their stay.

Edit Photos for Clarity and Brightness

Even well-shot photos can benefit from professional editing. Adjusting brightness, contrast, and sharpness can make your images look polished and professional. Avoid over-editing, as overly saturated or unrealistic photos may mislead guests.

Include Updated Seasonal or Themed Images

Refreshing your listing with seasonal or themed photos can cap- ture attention and keep your property relevant year-round. For example, show your cozy fireplace in winter or your blooming garden in spring to appeal to seasonal travelers.

Use Wide-Angle Lenses to Show Room Size

Wide-angle lenses can help capture the full scope of your rooms, making spaces appear more open and inviting. They're especially useful for smaller spaces, as they provide a more accurate representation of the layout.

Provide Accurate Captions for All Photos

Pair your photos with descriptive and accurate captions to guide potential guests through your property. Mention key features, such as "spacious living room with a 50-inch smart TV" or "modern kitchen equipped with stainless steel appliances."

Update Photos Regularly as the Property Changes

As your property evolves, so should your photos. If you've updated furniture, added amenities, or renovated, ensure your listing reflects these changes with new images to avoid misleading guests.

Showcase the Exterior and Surroundings

Don't limit your listing to interior shots. Highlight the property's exterior, including the entrance, outdoor spaces, and any unique features like a pool, garden, or balcony. Include surroundings like scenic views, proximity to attractions, or nearby amenities.

Highlight Unique Features in Detail

Unique features can set your property apart. Showcase special amenities like a cozy reading nook, luxury bathroom fixtures, or a fire pit area. Close-up shots of these features can make your listing more compelling.

High-quality photographs are a cornerstone of successful short-term vacation rental marketing. Guests rely on images to form their first impression of your property, and captivating photos can make the difference between securing a booking or losing out to competitors. By hiring a professional photographer, using natural light, staging your property, and keeping your images updated, you can present your rental in the best possible light. This investment enhances your property's appeal and drives higher occupancy rates and revenue.

Chapter 7- STVRO Problem #7: Negative Reviews and Inconsistent Guest Experiences

Overcoming Negative Reviews and Inconsistent Guest Experiences in Short-Term Rentals

In the competitive industry of short-term vacation rentals, guest satisfaction is crucial for sustaining and growing your business. Negative reviews and inconsistent guest experiences can quickly damage your property's reputation, discouraging potential guests and lowering your occupancy rates. To counter these challenges, it's essential to adopt proactive strategies that ensure every guest has a memorable and positive stay.

Address Complaints Promptly and Professionally

One of the most effective ways to manage negative reviews is to respond quickly and professionally. Acknowledge the guest's concerns, apologize if necessary, and offer a solution to rectify the issue. A prompt, empathetic response demonstrates your commitment to guest satisfaction and can turn a negative experience into a positive one.

Offer Discounts or Refunds for Bad Experiences

When guests have a subpar stay, offering discounts or partial refunds can help mend the relationship. This gesture shows that you value their feedback and are willing to make amends, which can lead to repeat bookings and even updated, more favorable reviews.

Provide Consistent Quality through Staff Training

Training your staff to deliver exceptional service is vital for creating a consistent guest experience. Ensure your team understands the importance of cleanliness, hospitality, and responsiveness. Regular training sessions can help reinforce standards and keep your staff aligned with your goals.

Regularly Update Amenities and Décor

Guests expect modern and well-maintained properties. Make it a priority to refresh your décor and update amenities to meet current trends and guest expectations. This not only enhances the guest experience but also demonstrates your attention to detail and willingness to invest in their comfort.

Standardize Check-In and Check-Out Procedures

A seamless check-in and check-out process can significantly

enhance guests' overall experiences. Standardize these procedures by providing clear instructions, offering keyless entry, and ensuring guests feel welcomed and informed from booking until their departure.

Follow Up with Guests Post-Stay for Feedback

Reaching out to guests after their stay to request feedback shows that you value their opinions. This also gives you an opportunity to address any issues privately before they escalate into public negative reviews.

Invest in Mystery Guest Evaluations

Consider hiring mystery guests to evaluate your property and services. These professionals provide unbiased insights into the guest experience, helping you identify areas for improvement that might not be immediately apparent.

Use Reviews to Identify Areas for Improvement

Negative reviews can be a valuable source of feedback. Analyze recurring complaints to pinpoint problem areas and develop strategies to address them. This proactive approach ensures continuous improvement.

Reward Guests Who Leave Positive Reviews

Encourage satisfied guests to leave positive reviews by offering incentives, such as discounts on future stays. This boosts your online reputation and fosters loyalty among your guests.

Implement a Hospitality Management System

Using a hospitality management system can streamline operations, manage bookings, and track guest preferences. These tools ensure consistency across all aspects of your rental business, leading to smoother operations and happier guests.

Negative reviews and inconsistent guest experiences can be detrimental to your short-term rental business, but they also provide opportunities for growth and improvement. By promptly addressing complaints, offering quality service, and utilizing guest feedback, you can create a consistently exceptional experience that keeps guests returning. With these strategies, your property will stand out in a crowded market, resulting in higher ratings, repeat bookings, and increased profitability.

Chapter 8- STVRO Problem #8: Regulatory and Legal Compliance

Navigating Regulatory and Legal Compliance for Short-Term Vacation Rentals

Owning and operating a short-term vacation rental property can be a rewarding venture, but navigating the regulatory and legal landscape is a crucial part of ensuring long-term success. Legal and compliance issues can result in fines, lawsuits, or even the shutdown of your rental if not properly managed. Implementing a comprehensive approach to compliance safeguards your business and fosters trust with your guests.

Stay Informed About Local Rental Laws

Short-term rental regulations vary widely between cities, counties, and states. Stay informed about the rules in your area by regularly checking local government websites or attending community meetings. This knowledge helps you avoid unintentional violations and ensures your property remains compliant.

Obtain All Necessary Permits and Licenses

Many jurisdictions require specific permits or licenses to operate a short-term rental. These can include business licenses, health permits, or occupancy permits. Ensure you apply for and renew these documents as required to maintain your legal standing.

Partner with a Legal Advisor or Consultant

Legal advisors or consultants specializing in short-term rentals can provide valuable guidance on navigating complex regulations. They can help you understand zoning requirements, tax obligations, and liability concerns, ensuring your business operates within the bounds of the law.

Display Clear Cancellation and Refund Policies

Transparent cancellation and refund policies protect both you and your guests. Clearly outline these terms on your booking platform and in guest communications. This not only meets legal requirements in many areas but also enhances your reputation for honesty and professionalism.

Ensure Tax Compliance

Short-term vacation rental hosts are often required to pay local occupancy taxes, sales taxes, or even income taxes on rental earnings. Use tax software or hire a tax professional to ensure accurate and timely payments. Some booking platforms also assist with automatic tax collection and remittance.

Create a Liability Waiver for Guests

A liability waiver is a vital document that limits your responsibility for accidents or damages occurring during a guest's stay. Work with a legal expert to draft a comprehensive waiver and ensure guests review and sign it before their stay.

Follow Zoning Regulations for Short-Term Rentals

Zoning laws can dictate where short-term rentals are permitted. Confirm that your property complies with these regulations and any restrictions on the number of guests, noise levels, or parking. Violating zoning laws can result in penalties or forced closure.

Install Security Features to Meet Local Safety Codes

Safety compliance is critical. Install smoke detectors, carbon monoxide alarms, fire extinguishers, and first aid kits. Verify that your property meets local safety codes, including clear emergency exits, proper lighting, and secure locks.

Participate in Landlord or Rental Owner Associations

Joining associations for landlords or rental property owners provides access to resources, networking, and updates on legal changes. These organizations can help you stay ahead of compliance requirements and learn from industry best practices.

Use Legal Templates for Rental Agreements

Rental agreements protect both parties by clearly defining expectations and responsibilities. Use professionally designed legal templates to ensure your agreements cover key aspects like payment terms, house rules, and liability clauses.

Maintaining regulatory and legal compliance is a critical part of running a successful short-term vacation rental. By staying informed, seeking professional guidance, and implementing robust legal practices, you can protect your business from risks and create a reliable, trustworthy experience for your guests. Compliance ensures your operations remain uninterrupted and enhances your property's reputation, contributing to long-term profitability.

Chapter 9- STVRO Problem #9: Damage or Theft

Mitigating Damage and Theft in Short-Term Rentals

As a short-term vacation rental owner, damage or theft is one of the most significant risks to your property and profitability. The unpredictable nature of guest behavior, coupled with the temporary nature of rentals, can sometimes lead to property damage, missing items, or even more severe theft. However, by implementing preventative measures and having a clear strategy in place, you can protect your investment and maintain a positive guest experience.

Require a Security Deposit

A security deposit is one of the most straightforward and effective ways to mitigate damage and theft. By holding a refundable deposit, guests are more likely to treat your property with care. The deposit can cover minor damages or missing items, compensating you for any unforeseen expenses. Make sure to outline the deposit terms clearly in your rental agreement and on your listing.

Install Security Cameras in Common Areas (If Permitted)

Security cameras can deter potential theft and help you monitor any possible incidents. Install cameras in common areas such as entryways, hallways, or parking lots, but ensure you follow local laws and disclose their presence to guests. This transparency reassures guests that their safety is a priority while safeguarding your property.

Offer Insurance Options for Guests

Offering insurance options to guests can help provide additional coverage for damage or theft. Many booking platforms allow hosts to offer insurance at the time of booking, giving guests peace of mind and protecting you against costly repairs or lost items. Insurance options can cover accidental damage, theft, or other incidents, reducing the risk of financial loss for both parties.

Use Durable and Replaceable Furnishings

Investing in durable, high-quality furniture and décor can reduce the likelihood of expensive damages. Consider materials that are more resistant to wear and tear, such as stain-resistant fabrics or solid wood furniture. Additionally, choose furnishings that are easily replaceable or can be cleaned easily to minimize the financial impact of damage.

Conduct Thorough Inventory Checks

Before and after each guest stay, conduct a thorough inventory check to ensure that all items are accounted for. Document the condition of your property and its contents with photos and written records. This helps identify any missing or damaged items quickly, which is essential for resolving issues with guests in a timely manner.

Screen Guests Through Booking Platforms

Booking platforms offer various tools to help screen potential guests, such as reviews, verified profiles, and guest history. By reviewing these details, you can get a better sense of who is renting your property. Many platforms also offer host guarantees, adding an extra layer of protection against damage or theft.

Provide Clear House Rules

Establish clear and comprehensive house rules for your guests, outlining expectations for behavior, property care, and any prohibited activities. Be sure to emphasize the consequences of damage or theft in these rules. By setting boundaries upfront, guests will understand their responsibilities, which can lead to more respectful and careful behavior.

Invest in Theft-Deterrent Technologies

Security technologies such as smart locks, motion sensors, and alarm systems can help prevent unauthorized access or theft. Smart locks also allow you to control guest access remotely, which can be helpful if you suspect that an unauthorized guest may be staying on your property. These technologies offer peace of mind, knowing you can monitor your property in real-time.

Keep Valuables Locked or Removed

Remove or securely lock away valuable items such as electronics, jewelry, or sensitive documents before guests arrive. If these items are not essential for the guest experience, keeping them out of sight is best to prevent temptation. By minimizing the risk of theft, you can focus on providing a great guest experience without worry.

Build Relationships with Local Authorities

Establishing a good relationship with local authorities, including law enforcement and neighborhood watch groups, can help you quickly address any potential issues of theft or vandalism. Being known as a responsible, law-abiding host will also strengthen your standing in the local community and can act as a deterrent for guests who may consider inappropriate actions.

Damage and theft are unfortunate realities of managing a short-term vacation rental, but they don't have to be inevitable. By implementing preventive measures such as security deposits, clear house rules, and theft-deterrent technologies, you can reduce the likelihood of these issues. Moreover, regular property checks, inventory management, and screening guests effectively further safeguard your property. With the right precautions in place, you can focus on providing exceptional experiences for your guests while protecting your investment and ensuring the long-term success of your short-term rental business.

Chapter 10- STVRO Problem #10: Safety and Accessibility

Ensuring Safety and Accessibility in Short-Term Rentals

Safety and accessibility are fundamental to providing a positive and secure guest experience in your short-term **vacation** rental property. As a host, it is your responsibility to create an environment where guests feel safe, comfortable, and at ease throughout their stay. Addressing safety and accessibility concerns not only fosters positive reviews but also protects your guests, yourself, and your business from potential liabilities.

Install Smoke and Carbon Monoxide Detectors

One of the most critical safety measures for any rental property is the installation of smoke and carbon monoxide detectors. These life-saving devices alert guests to fire or carbon monoxide leaks, providing essential time to evacuate the building. Make sure detectors are installed in every bedroom, hallway, and common area. Regularly check and maintain these devices to ensure they're functioning properly, as a failure to do so can lead to serious consequences.

Provide Clear Emergency Contact Information

Make sure that all guests have easy access to emergency contact information. This includes local emergency services (police, fire, medical) and your contact details as the host. Consider placing this information prominently within the rental property, such as in a guest manual or on the wall near the entrance. Clear communication of emergency numbers gives guests peace of mind and ensures they can act quickly in a crisis.

Ensure Easy Access for First Responders

In the event of an emergency, it's essential that first responders can access your property quickly. Make sure the address is visible from the street and that no obstructions are blocking the front door or pathways. If your rental is in a building or complex, provide clear instructions on how first responders can reach the unit. Accessibility in emergencies could save precious time and lives.

Add Accessibility Features like Ramps and Grab Bars

Making your property accessible to all guests, including those with mobility challenges, is a legal responsibility and a thoughtful service in some areas. Adding features like ramps, grab bars in the bathroom, and wider doorways ensures that guests with disabilities can enjoy a safe stay. Additionally, accessible bathroom and kitchen setups should be considered, which can further enhance the comfort of guests with mobility impairments.

Provide a Well-Stocked First-Aid Kit

A well-stocked first-aid kit is essential in any rental property. Include bandages, antiseptics, gauze, pain relievers, and any other common medical supplies. Ensure the kit is easily accessible, and consider providing a list of first-aid instructions or guidelines for common injuries. This small gesture adds a layer of security, especially for families or groups with children.

Regularly Inspect for Safety Hazards

Routine inspections are essential to maintaining a safe rental property. Check for any safety hazards such as loose handrails, faulty wiring, or exposed nails. Look for signs of mold, uneven flooring, or any other potential dangers that could pose a risk to guests. Identifying and addressing hazards promptly can prevent accidents and ensure a safe environment for all visitors.

Use Non-Slip Rugs and Flooring

Slips and falls are a common cause of injuries in rental properties. To reduce the risk, use non-slip rugs and flooring throughout the property, especially in areas that may become wet, such as bathrooms, kitchens, and hallways. Non-slip mats in showers and bathtubs are also a simple way to prevent accidents. These proactive steps can make a significant difference in creating a safe and comfortable environment.

Offer Clear Signage for Emergency Exits

Clear signage for emergency exits is vital, particularly in multi-story properties or buildings with more complex layouts. Mark emergency exits with easily visible signs and ensure they are free from obstruction. In case of an emergency, guests need to know where to go quickly, and clear signage reduces confusion and panic during critical moments.

Test Safety Equipment Regularly

Safety equipment, such as fire extinguishers, alarms, and sprinklers, should be regularly tested to ensure they are in working order. Schedule routine maintenance and inspections for all safety devices, ensuring they are up to code and capable of protecting your guests in case of emergency. Regular testing prevents malfunctions that could put guests at risk.

Provide Accessible Parking Spaces

If your rental property includes parking, make sure to provide accessible parking spaces for guests who may need them. Ensure these spaces are clearly marked, close to the entrance, and free from obstacles. Accessibility for guests with mobility challenges should extend beyond the property's interior, making it easier for them to access their accommodations safely.

Ensuring the safety and accessibility of your short-term vacation rental is crucial for providing a positive guest experience and maintaining a successful business. By installing smoke detectors, offering emergency contact information, and addressing accessibility needs, you can create a safe environment for all guests. Regular inspections, non-slip rugs, and well-marked emergency exits further minimize risks while providing accessible parking and amenities ensures inclusivity. Investing in safety and accessibility measures protects your guests and strengthens your reputation as a responsible, thoughtful host.

Chapter 11- STVRO Problem #11: High Operating Costs

Managing High Operating Costs in Short-Term Rentals

Operating a successful short-term vacation rental property comes with many responsibilities, but one of the most challenging aspects is managing high operating costs. From utility bills to maintenance, these expenses can quickly add up, impacting profitability. However, there are several strategies you can implement to reduce costs while maintaining a high level of service for your guests. This chapter will cover some solutions to help manage and lower your operating costs in the short-term rental industry.

Invest in Energy-Efficient Appliances

One of the largest contributors to high operating costs is energy consumption. To mitigate this, invest in energy-efficientc appliances such asc refrigerators, cdishwashers, and washing machines. These appliances use less energy while providing the same level of service, helping to reduce electricity and water bills over time. While the initial investment may be higher, the long-term savings make this a smart financial decision for property owners.

Use Smart Thermostats to Reduce Energy Use

Another way to lower energy costs is by installing smart thermostats. These devices allow you to program temperature settings based on occupancy patterns, ensuring that energy isn't wasted when the property is unoccupied. For example, you can set the thermostat to lower the temperature during the winter or raise it during the summer when the property is empty. This level of control reduces overall heating and cooling costs, which can otherwise be a significant expense.

Negotiate Bulk Rates for Cleaning Supplies

Cleaning costs can be another major expense, especially for larger properties or properties with frequent turnover. A great way to save money here is to negotiate bulk rates for cleaning supplies. Purchasing items like toilet paper, detergents, and cleaning agents in bulk not only ensures you're stocked up but also reduces the cost per unit. Many suppliers offer discounts for larger orders, leading to substantial savings over time.

Automate Processes to Save Labor Costs

Automation is one of the best ways to reduce labor costs and streamline operations in a short-term rental business. Implementing automated systems for guest communication, booking confirmations, check-ins, and check-outs can save you time and money. There are numerous software solutions available that can manage these tasks without requiring constant attention, reducing the need for manual work and ensuring that your property is running efficiently.

Regularly Review Operating Expenses

It's essential to regularly review your operating expenses to identify areas where you can cut costs. Whether it's subscriptions to booking platforms, service fees, or unexpected repairs, regularly assessing your expenses will help you spot unnecessary or excessive spending. Once identified, you can take steps to renegotiate contracts, find alternative providers, or eliminate non-essential services. Regular financial reviews will also help you forecast and plan for future expenses, allowing you to maintain a healthy cash flow.

Offer Seasonal Pricing to Ensure Steady Revenue

Seasonal pricing is another strategy to help balance out fluctuations in occupancy and maintain steady revenue throughout the year. By adjusting your rates to match demand, you can ensure higher occupancy during peak seasons while attracting guests during off-peak times with discounted rates.

Offering seasonal pricing helps you maximize your revenue potential while maintaining a competitive edge in a market where demand can vary widely.

Outsource Non-Essential Tasks

As a short-term vacation rental owner, it's important to focus on the tasks that directly contribute to your revenue. Outsourcing non-essential tasks such as landscaping, bookkeeping, or administrative duties can help you save time and reduce operating costs. By hiring professionals or using third-party services for these tasks, you can free up your time to focus on guest experience and other key areas that drive profitability.

Partner with Other Property Owners for Shared Costs

Collaborating with other property owners in your area can be an effective way to share costs and reduce expenses. You can pool resources for things like bulk cleaning supplies, maintenance services, or even marketing campaigns. Sharing these costs helps to reduce the financial burden of operating multiple properties while fostering a sense of community among local property owners.

Refinance Loans to Reduce Interest Rates

For many short-term vacation rental owners, loan payments can be a significant ongoing expense. If you have a mortgage on your property, refinancing your loan to secure a lower interest rate can help reduce your monthly payments. This can result in substantial savings over the long term, freeing up capital that can be reinvested into your property or used to cover other operating costs.

Use Occupancy Data to Optimize Staffing

Staffing costs can quickly add up, especially if you're over-staffing during slow periods or underestimating staffing needs duringbusytimes. Byusingoccupancydataandbooking trends, you can optimize your staffing levels to match demand. This ensures that you're not paying for unnecessary labor during off-peak times while being adequately staffed during high-demand periods. Utilizing software to track booking patterns can help you make data-driven decisions about when to schedule cleaning crews, maintenance workers, or other staff.

Managing high operating costs is a critical part of maintaining profitability in the short-term rental industry. By implementing these solutions—ranging from energy-efficient appliances to outsourcing non-essential tasks—you can reduce your expenses while ensuring a high-quality guest experience. Regularly reviewing your expenses and using technology to optimize operations will help you stay on top of your costs, allowing you to reinvest in your property and grow your rental business. By applying these strategies, you'll not only reduce your operating expenses but also improve your overall bottom line, ensuring long-term success in the competitive short-term rental market.

Chapter 12- STVRO Problem #12: Time Management and Overwhelm

Time Management and Overwhelm in Short-Term Rentals: Effective Solutions for Efficiency

Managing a short-term vacation rental property can often feel overwhelming, especially as your business grows and the demands increase. From guest communication and bookings to cleaning and maintenance, the responsibilities can quickly pile up. Without proper time management strategies in place, it's easy to become overwhelmed. Fortunately, there are several effective solutions that can help you streamline operations, save time, and reduce stress, enabling you to balance your personal and professional life.

Hire a Property Manager

One of the most effective ways to manage the time-consuming tasks of running a short-term rental is to hire a property manager. Property managers handle everything from guest communication to maintenance, allowing you to offload day-to-day operations. By outsourcing these responsibilities, you can focus on other aspects of your business or personal life without worrying about the constant demands of property management.

Use Property Management Software for Scheduling

Property management software is an invaluable tool for organizing and automating the scheduling of various tasks. These platforms offer features that allow you to manage bookings, check-ins, check-outs, and maintenance schedules all in one place. With an integrated calendar and task management system, you can easily track bookings, coordinate cleaning and maintenance, and ensure that everything runs smoothly, saving you significant time and effort.

Automate Guest Communications and Payments

Automating guest communications is one of the most effective ways to save time and reduce overwhelm. By using automation tools, you can set up pre-written messages for booking confirmations, check-in instructions, reminders, and check-out instructions. Additionally, automating payments ensures that you don't need to manually process transactions, giving you more time to focus on other aspects of your business. This reduces your workload and ensures consistent and timely communication with your guests.

Delegate Cleaning and Maintenance Tasks

Cleaning and maintenance are some of the most labor-intensive tasks in property management. Instead of handling these tasks yourself, delegate them to professionals. Hire a reliable cleaning crew to handle turnover, deep cleanings, and regular maintenance tasks. By outsourcing these responsibilities, you free up your time to focus on guest experience, marketing, or managing other properties in your portfolio.

Create a Daily, Weekly, and Monthly Task Schedule

Establishing a clear and structured task schedule is crucial for managing time effectively. Break down your responsibilities into daily, weekly, and monthly tasks, and prioritize them based on urgency. This helps you stay organized, reduces the risk of missing important deadlines, and ensures your rental is always prepared for guests. A well-organized schedule will also give you a better sense of control over your workload and help you avoid feeling overwhelmed.

Outsource Marketing and Social Media Management

Marketing and social media management can be time-consuming, but they are essential for attracting guests to your property. If you're finding it difficult to keep up with creating posts, responding to messages, and managing ads, consider outsourcing these tasks to a digital marketing expert or social media manager. They can help you create a content strategy, schedule posts, engage with potential guests, and run advertising campaigns, allowing you to focus on other areas of your business.

Use a Virtual Assistant for Administrative Tasks

A virtual assistant (VA) can be a valuable asset to your short-term vacation rental business. VAs can handle various administrative tasks, such as responding to inquiries, managing emails, organizing bookings, and dealing with guest issues. By hiring a VA, you can delegate routine tasks and focus on higher-priority activities, such as expanding your property portfolio or improving guest services.

Batch Tasks to Save Time

Batching tasks is a simple but effective time management technique. Instead of switching between different tasks throughout the day, group similar tasks together and complete them in one go. For example, set aside a specific time each day to respond to guest inquiries or handle all guest check-in instructions at once. This minimizes distractions and increases productivity, allowing you to focus on more important or high-value activities.

Set Boundaries for Work-Life Balance

Running a short-term vacation rental can often blur the line between work and personal life. To avoid burnout, it's essential to set clear boundaries. Establish specific working hours for handling guest communications and property management tasks. Outside of these hours, turn off notifications and dedicate time to personal activities, family, and relaxation. By setting boundaries, you'll maintain a healthier work-life balance and prevent feeling constantly overwhelmed.

Take Advantage of Time Management Tools Like Calendars and Apps

Lastly, take advantage of time management tools like digital calendars and task management apps. Tools like Google Calendar, Trello, or Asana allow you to schedule tasks, set reminders, and track your progress. These apps can help you stay on top of your to-do list, reduce clutter, and ensure that nothing falls through the cracks. With real-time syncing, these tools allow you to manage tasks and bookings from any location, keeping everything organized and efficient.

Time management is critical for running a successful short-term vacation rental business without feeling overwhelmed. By hiring a property manager, automating guest communications, delegating tasks, and implementing time management strategies, you can streamline your operations and reduce stress. Establishing a daily, weekly, and monthly schedule, outsourcing marketing, and using technology will help you maintain control of your business while keeping your work-life balance intact. With the right tools and strategies in place, you can achieve long-term success without burning out.

Conclusion

Managing a short-term vacation rental can feel overwhelming, but it doesn't have to be. In Rental Roadblocks, we've explored some of the most common challenges that rental owners face and provided practical, actionable solutions to tackle each one. Whether you're dealing with low occupancy rates, negative reviews, property maintenance issues, or the complexities of legal compliance, there are strategies you can implement to improve your business and increase your profitability.

As we've seen throughout this book, success in the short-term rental industry is all about preparation, adaptability, and a commitment to continually improving your property and guest experience. By taking a proactive approach to addressing issues like poor communication, outdated photos, or lackluster amenities, you can create a rental that attracts more guests and generates higher revenue. Moreover, staying organized, utilizing technology, and streamlining processes can help you manage your property more efficiently, reducing the time and effort required to keep things running smoothly.

One of the key takeaways from this book is the importance of staying informed and adaptable. The short-term vacation rental market is dynamic and ever-evolving, with guest expectations constantly shifting and new trends emerging regularly. To stay competitive, you need to keep your finger on the pulse of industry changes and be ready to pivot your strategy when necessary. Whether by offering personalized guest experiences, investing in luxury amenities, or leveraging new marketing tools, staying ahead of the curve will help ensure your rental business thrives in an increasingly crowded market.

By addressing the 12 roadblocks discussed in this book, you'll not only improve your bottom line but also create a positive, memorable experience for your guests. When guests have a great experience at your property, they're more likely to leave positive reviews, return for future stays, and recommend your rental to others. This kind of word-of-mouth marketing is invaluable and can lead to a steady stream of bookings and long- term success.

In conclusion, overcoming the challenges of short-term rental ownership is entirely possible, and with the right strategies in place, you can turn these roadblocks into opportunities for growth and improvement. Armed with the solutions provided in this book, you're now better equipped to tackle the issues that may have been holding your rental business back. Whether it's optimizing pricing, improving guest communication, or making your property stand out with professional photos, the steps you take today will help ensure a brighter, more profitable future for your rental business.

Remember, success in short-term rentals isn't just about managing your property—it's about providing an experience that guests will remember, talk about, and come back for. Now, it's time to put the knowledge you've gained into action and watch your rental business rise to new heights.

It's time to pass on your thoughts and show other readers where they can find this book.

Simply by leaving your honest opinion of your purchase on Amazon, you'll show others where they can find books and products they may be interested in.

Thank you for your help!

Scan code to leave a review on Amazon

Short-Term Vacation Rental Common Terms and Definitions

Amenities
Features provided to enhance guest comfort, such as Wi-Fi, a pool, or kitchen supplies.

Availability Calendar
A tool that shows the dates a property is available for booking.

Back-to-Back Booking
Two consecutive guest reservations without a gap between them.

Base Rate
The standard nightly rate for a property before discounts or fees.

Booking Confirmation
A notification sent to a guest to confirm their reservation.

Booking Fee

A fee charged by a platform or property owner for processing a reservation.

Cancellation Policy

Rules outlining the conditions under which a guest can cancel a booking and receive a refund.

Check-In

The process of a guest arriving and gaining access to the rental property.

Check-Out

The process of a guest leaving the property at the end of their stay.

Cleaning Fee

A charge for preparing the property for the next guest, covering cleaning services.

Co-Hosting

When multiple individuals manage a short-term rental property together.

Damage Deposit

A refundable amount collected from guests to cover potential damages.

Dynamic Pricing

A strategy that adjusts nightly rates based on demand, season, and other factors.

Extended Stay

A reservation lasting longer than the typical duration, often with discounted rates.

Furnished Rental

A property equipped with furniture, appliances, and other necessities for guest use.

Guest Experience

The overall impression a guest has during their stay, influenced by service, amenities, and comfort.

Guest Manual

A guide provided to guests with property rules, local tips, and instructions for using amenities.

House Rules

Guidelines set by the property owner that guests must follow during their stay.

Instant Booking

A feature allowing guests to book without waiting for host approval.

Keyless Entry

A system allowing guests to access the property using a code or digital key.

Late Check-Out

An option allowing guests to leave later than the standard check-out time.

Listing Description
The written overview of a property on a booking platform, including features and amenities.

Local Partnerships
Collaborations with area businesses, like restaurants or tour operators, to enhance guest stays.

Long-Term Rental
A lease agreement typically lasting more than 30 days.

Loyalty Program
A system that rewards repeat guests with discounts or perks.

Market Saturation
A condition where a large number of rental properties compete in the same area.

Marketing Strategy
A plan to attract guests through advertising, branding, and promotions.

Mid-Stay Cleaning
A cleaning service provided during a guest's extended stay.

Minimum Stay Requirement
The shortest duration a guest must book a property.

Multilingual Support
Customer service provided in multiple languages to accommodate international guests.

No-Show
A guest who does not arrive for their reservation without canceling.

Off-Season
A period of low demand for rentals in a particular area.

Occupancy Rate
The percentage of time a property is rented out compared to its total availability.

Online Travel Agency (OTA)
A platform like Airbnb or Booking.com used to list and book rental properties.

Outdoor Amenities
Features such as fire pits, grills, or pools located outside the property.

Overbooking
When a property is mistakenly booked for the same dates by multiple guests.

Payment Processor
A service that facilitates online payments for bookings.

Peak Season
The time of year when demand for rentals is highest.

Pet-Friendly Rental
A property that allows guests to bring their pets.

Pricing Strategy
The method used to set nightly rates to maximize revenue.

Property Inspection
A routine check to ensure the rental is in good condition.

Property Manager
A professional responsible for overseeing the operations of a rental property.

Referral Program
A system that rewards guests for referring new customers.

Refund Policy
The terms under which a guest may receive their money back after canceling a reservation.

Repeat Guest
A customer who has stayed at the property multiple times.

Revenue Management
The practice of optimizing rental income through pricing and occupancy strategies.

Seasonal Pricing
Variable rates depending on the time of year.

Security Deposit
A refundable fee collected to cover potential damages or extra cleaning.

Self-Check-In
A feature allowing guests to access the property without host assistance.

Short-Term Rental
A property rented for a period typically less than 30 days.

Smart Home Technology
Devices like smart locks and thermostats used to enhance the guest experience.

Split Payment
A feature allowing guests to divide the cost of a booking among multiple payers.

Staging
The process of arranging furniture and décor to make a property more appealing.

STVRO
Short-Term Vacation Rental Owner

Superhost
A designation given by platforms like Airbnb to highly rated and experienced hosts.

Target Audience
The specific group of travelers a rental property aims to attract.

Tax Compliance

The process of meeting legal obligations for paying taxes on rental income.

Terms and Conditions

The rules and guidelines governing a guest's use of the rental property.

Travel Insurance

A policy covering unexpected events like cancellations or emergencies during a trip.

Upselling

Encouraging guests to purchase additional services or upgrades.

Vacation Rental

A property rented out to travelers for leisure purposes.

Virtual Assistant

A remote worker handling administrative tasks for a rental business.

Walkthrough Video

A virtual tour showing the layout and features of a property.

Welcome Basket

A complimentary assortment of snacks or local goods provided to guests upon arrival.

Wide-Angle Lens

A camera lens used to capture expansive views of a property's interior or exterior.

Wi-Fi Speed

The internet connection speed available at the rental property.

Short-Term Vacation Rental and Hosting Resources

Here's a comprehensive list of resources for short-term vacation rental owners, including websites, tools, and organizations that can help improve operations, boost revenue, and enhance guest experiences:

General Information & Industry News

- Vacation Rental Management Association (VRMA): Industry updates, conferences, and resources for vacation rental professionals.
- https://www.vrma.org/
- ShortTermRentalz: Newsandinsightsspecifictotheshort-term rental industry.
- https://shorttermrentalz.com/
- Skift: Travel industry insights, including short-term rentals.
- https://skift.com/

- AirDNA Blog: Analytics, data trends, and tips for vacation rental hosts.
- https://www.airdna.co/blog

Pricing Tools

- PriceLabs: Dynamic pricing software to optimize rental rates.
- https://www.usepricelabs.com/
- Beyond Pricing: Revenue management and pricing automation platform.
- https://www.beyondpricing.com/
- Wheelhouse: Pricing optimization for vacation rentals.
- https://www.usewheelhouse.com/

Property Management Software (PMS)

- Hostfully: A property management platform with automation tools and a digital guidebook feature.
- https://www.hostfully.com/
- Guesty: Comprehensive PMS for managing bookings, communications, and operations.
- https://www.guesty.com/
- Tokeet: Manage bookings, channels, and guest communications in one platform.
- https://www.tokeet.com/
- Lodgify: Build a website, manage bookings, and integrate with OTAs.
- https://www.lodgify.com/

Cleaning & Maintenance Services

- TurnoverBnB: Schedule cleanings and manage cleaners automatically.
- https://turnoverbnb.com/
- Handy: Book cleaning and handyman services quickly.
- https://www.handy.com/

Marketing Tools

- Canva: Design custom graphics for marketing your rental property.
- https://www.canva.com/
- Mailchimp: Email marketing platform to engage guests and build a subscriber list.
- https://mailchimp.com/
- Buffer: Social media scheduling to promote your property.
- https://buffer.com/
- Facebook Business: Create ads and target potential guests.
- https://business.facebook.com/

Guest Communication

- Breezeway: Guest messaging and operations management tool.
- https://www.breezeway.io/
- Automate Guest Reviews: Tools like Smartbnb (Hospitable) streamline guest communications.

- https://www.hospitable.com/
- Airbnb Message Templates: Downloadable templates for consistent communication.

Revenue Management & Analytics

- AirDNA:Market data, analytics, and insights for short-term rentals.
- https://www.airdna.co/
- Key Data Dashboard: Benchmark your rental performance against market trends.
- https://www.keydatadashboard.com/

Listing Platforms

- Airbnb: A leading platform to list and manage vacation rentals.
- https://www.airbnb.com/
- Vrbo: Platform for vacation homes, cabins, and unique stays.
- https://www.vrbo.com/
- Booking.com: Listing platform for vacation rentals and hotels.
- https://www.booking.com/

Security & Safety

- Minut: Noise monitoring to protect your property and

neighbors.
- https://www.minut.com/
- Ring: Smart doorbells and cameras for added security.
- https://ring.com/
- NoiseAware: Detect and prevent noise disturbances.
- https://www.noiseaware.com/

Educational Resources

- BiggerPockets: A real estate investment community with rental resources.
- https://www.biggerpockets.com/
- STR Hub: Tips and strategies for vacation rental success.
- https://strhub.com/

Energy Efficiency

- Nest: Smart thermostats for energy savings.
- https://store.google.com/
- Sense: Energy monitoring for your vacation rental.
- https://sense.com/

Find Property Management Templates, Printable Welcome Signs, Hosting Guides, Checklists, and even more resources for Short-Term Vacation Renal Owners in my Etsy Shop - Otis Design Boutique.

Apps for Short-Term Vacation Rental Owners

Managing a short-term vacation rental or rental property management business can be streamlined with the right applications.

Below is a curated list of apps designed to enhance various aspects of property management, from booking and guest communication to maintenance and financial tracking.

AirGMS (iGMS)
A comprehensive property management software that automates guest communication, booking management, and cleaning schedules. Features include multi-platform synchronization and financial reporting.
  https://www.igms.com/

AppFolio Property Manager
A cloud-based solution offering tools for marketing, leasing,

accounting, and maintenance management.Includes online pay-ment processing and a mobile app for on-the-go management.

https://www.appfolio.com/

Beyond Pricing

An automated dynamic pricing tool that adjusts rental rates based on market demand, local events, and seasonal trends to maximize revenue.

https://www.beyondpricing.com/

BookingSync

A property management system that synchronizes bookings across multiple platforms, manages guest relationships, and offers a website builder for direct bookings.

https://www.bookingsync.com/

Breezeway

A property operations platform focusing on cleaning and maintenance management, offering task scheduling, quality assurance, and mobile checklists.

https://www.breezeway.io/

Buildium

Designed for property managers, Buildium provides tools for accounting, tenant and lease tracking, and maintenance management, with a resident portal for online payments.

https://www.buildium.com/

Checkmate

An app that streamlines the check-in process by automating guest communications and providing digital registration forms.

https://www.checkmate.io/

Cloudbeds
A hospitality management suite that integrates property management, channel management, and booking engine functionalities, suitable for short-term rentals and boutique hotels.
https://www.cloudbeds.com/

Codedoor
A smart lock solution that allows property managers to provide guests with unique access codes, enhancing security and simplifying check-ins.
https://www.codedoor.com/

DoorLoop
An all-in-one property management software that offers features like tenant screening, lease management, accounting, and maintenance tracking.
https://www.doorloop.com/

DPGO
A dynamic pricing tool that uses AI to optimize rental rates based on market data, competitor analysis, and property performance.
https://www.dpgo.com/

Duve
Enhances guest experience by providing a personalized guest app, automated communication, and upselling opportunities.
https://www.duve.com/

Escapia
A comprehensive vacation rental software offering reservation management, trust accounting, and real-time owner reporting.
https://www.escapia.com/

Fetchit
An inventory and supply management app that helps hosts track and replenish items like toiletries, linens, and cleaning supplies.
https://fetchitapp.com/

Guesty
A property management platform that centralizes operations, including booking management, guest communication, and task automation.
https://www.guesty.com/

HomeAdvisor
A platform that connects property managers with local professionals for maintenance, repairs, and upgrades.
https://www.homeadvisor.com/

Hospitable (formerly Smartbnb)
Automates guest messaging, reviews, and task assignments, helping hosts manage multiple listings efficiently.
https://www.hospitable.com/

Hostaway
A vacation rental management software that integrates with major booking platforms, offering features like channel man-

agement, automated messaging, and analytics.

https://www.hostaway.com/

Keycafe

A key management system that allows property managers to securely share keys with guests and service providers through smart key lockers.

https://www.keycafe.com/

Kigo

A vacation rental software offering channel management, booking engine, and revenue management tools to optimize property performance.

https://www.kigo.net/

Lodgable

A distribution platform that helps property managers list their rentals on multiple OTAs while managing bookings and guest communications.

https://www.lodgable.com/

Lodgify

Provides a website builder, booking system, and channel manager, enabling hosts to accept direct bookings and manage reservations.

https://www.lodgify.com/

NoiseAware

A noise monitoring solution that alerts property managers to potential disturbances, helping prevent noise complaints and property damage.

https://www.noiseaware.com/

Operto

Offers smart home automation solutions, including keyless entry, energy management, and noise monitoring, enhancing guest experience and operational efficiency.

https://www.operto.com/

OwnerRez

A booking management system that integrates with major listing sites, offering features like guest communication, payment processing, and reporting.

https://www.ownerreservations.com/

Payfully

Provides hosts with advances on upcoming bookings, offering financial flexibility for property improvements or operational expenses.

https://www.payfully.co/

PriceLabs

A dynamic pricing tool that analyzes market data to recommend optimal pricing strategies, helping maximize occupancy and revenue.

https://www.usepricelabs.com/

Proper Insurance

Provides tailored insurance for vacation rental properties, covering property damage, liability, and loss of income.

https://www.proper.insure/

Properly

A cleaning and operations platform that offers visual check-lists, scheduling, and quality assurance tools for property man-agers and cleaners.

https://www.getproperly.com/

Rentec Direct

A property management software that provides tools for ten-ant screening, online rent collection, and accounting, making it ideal for landlords and property managers.

https://www.rentecdirect.com/

Rentredi

A user-friendly property management app for landlords, offering features like tenant screening, maintenance tracking, and rent collection.

https://www.rentredi.com/

ResMan

A property management platform offering accounting, com-pliance tools, maintenance tracking, and a resident portal for payments and communications.

https://www.myresman.com/

RoomRaccoon

An all-in-one property management system with booking engine, channel management, and payment processing for vacation rentals and boutique hotels.

https://roomraccoon.com/

Safely

A platform offering guest screening and insurance solutions to protect short-term rental properties from risks and liabilities.
https://safely.com/

Showplace

Helps short-term rental hosts add sponsored products and amenities to their properties while earning additional income.
https://www.showplacehq.com/

Smoobu

A property management software that synchronizes bookings, automates guest communications, and offers a booking website builder.
https://www.smoobu.com/

StayFi

Provides branded Wi-Fi login pages, enabling property managers to collect guest emails for marketing and engagement purposes.
https://stayfi.com/

Streamline

A vacation rental software offering tools for reservation management, marketing, and reporting, with integrations for third-party platforms.
https://www.streamlinevrs.com/

Superhog

A trust and safety platform offering guest verification and damage protection for short-term rental hosts.
https://www.superhog.com/

TaskRabbit
Connects property managers with local service providers for tasks like maintenance, repairs, and assembly.
https://www.taskrabbit.com/

Tokeet
A property management platform designed for small to mid-sized rental businesses, with features like booking management, channel management, and invoicing.
https://www.tokeet.com/

TurnoverBnB
An app that connects vacation rental hosts with cleaners, automates scheduling, and provides detailed checklists for cleaning tasks.
https://turnoverbnb.com/

Vacasa
A vacation rental management company with an owner app that provides real-time revenue tracking, booking updates, and property performance insights.
https://www.vacasa.com/

VacayMyWay
A vacation rental platform that empowers property owners with direct booking options, providing an alternative to mainstream OTAs.
https://www.vacaymyway.com/

Wheelhouse
A pricing optimization tool that analyzes data to set dynamic

rental rates, helping hosts maximize revenue and occupancy.
https://www.usewheelhouse.com/

Your Porter App

A mobile-first property management app for vacation rentals, offering channel management, automated messaging, and a direct booking website builder.
https://yourporter.com/

Zibo

A financial platform for landlords that offers tools for rent collection, banking, and insurance, with a focus on simplifying property management finances.
https://www.zibo.com/

Zeevou

A property management software that automates guest communication, direct bookings, and financial reporting, with a focus on operational efficiency.
https://zeevou.com/

Zoho CRM

A versatile customer relationship management tool that can be tailored for guest communications, booking management, and marketing.
https://www.zoho.com/crm/

Zumper

A rental listing platform with features like tenant screening, rent collection, and property marketing, helping hosts fill vacancies quickly.
https://www.zumper.com/

Take Your Short-Term Rental to the Next Level!

Congratulations on investing in your success as a short-term rental owner!

Managing a rental property can be rewarding, but maximizing your revenue while minimizing stress takes the right strategies, tools, and support.

That's where I come in.

Explore More Resources & Services

Beyond this book, I offer a variety of services, tools, and expert guidance designed to help rental owners like you enhance their listings, streamline operations, and boost bookings.

Whether you need insider tips, automation strategies, or personalized consulting, I've got you covered!

Cohosting Opportunities: Let's Work Together!

Want to maximize your rental's potential without the daily hassle? As a cohost and rental consultant, I work with property owners to increase amenities, enhance guest satisfaction, and optimize booking rates—all while ensuring you earn more with less effort.

Whether you're looking for expert guidance, hands-on support, or done-for-you solutions, I'm here to help.

Ready to take the next step?

Get in Touch Today!

Visit <u>Revenue Rise</u> for more resources & cohosting details

Your rental has incredible potential—let's unlock it together!